KT-455-003

contents

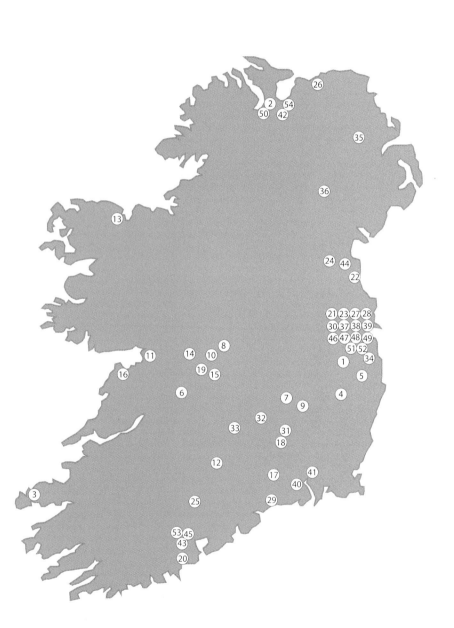

1   Cairn at Seefin, Co. Wicklow, c.3,000 BC
2   The Grianan of Aileach, Co. Donegal, c.100
3   Gallarus Oratory, Co. Kerry, c.8th century
4   Aghowle Church, Co. Wicklow, 9th century
5   Teampull Mhuire, Co. Wicklow, 10th century
6   St Cronan's Church, Co. Clare, 10th century
7   Timahoe Round Tower, Co. Laois, c.1150
8   The Nun's Church, Co. Offaly, 1167
9   Killeshin Church, Co. Laois, 12th century
10   Clonfert Cathedral, Co. Galway, from 11th century
11   Drumacoo Church, Co. Galway, c.1220
12   The Priory of St Edmund, Co. Tipperary, c.1260
13   Rosserk Abbey, Co. Mayo, c.1441
14   The Priory of St Mary, Co. Galway, c.1471
15   Lorrha, Co. Tipperary, 13th–15th centuries
16   Rathborney Church, Co. Clare, c.1500
17   Carrick Castle, Co. Tipperary, c.1565
18   Shee Alms House, Kilkenny, 1582
19   Portumna Castle, Co. Galway, c.1618
20   Southwell Gift Houses, Co. Cork, 1682
21   The Royal Hospital, Dublin, 1684
22   Beaulieu, Co. Louth, c.1700
23   Dr Steevens's Hospital, Dublin, 1733
24   Knock Abbey, or Thomastown Castle, Co. Louth, c.1770
25   King's Square, Co. Cork, 1780
26   Mussenden Temple, Co. Derry, c.1785
27   63 Merrion Square, Dublin, 1791
28   Kilmainham Gaol, Dublin, 1796
29   Cove Cottage, Co. Waterford, c.1810
30   The King's Inns, Dublin, 1817
31   Bridge House, Kilkenny, c.1820
32   Lacy's Public House, Co. Kilkenny, 1825
33   Presentation Convent, Co. Tipperary, 1826
34   Forge at Enniskerry, Co. Wicklow, c.1830
35   First Presbyterian Church, Antrim, 1837
36   Former Belfast Bank, Armagh, 1850
37   Broadstone Station, Dublin, 1850
38   University Church, Dublin, 1855
39   The Museum Building, Dublin, 1857
40   Waterford City Post Office, 1879
41   Shop at New Ross, Co. Wexford, c.1880
42   The Guildhall, Derry, 1887
43   The Honan Chapel, Cork, 1916
44   House at Collon, Co. Louth, c.1920
45   The Church of Christ the King, Cork, 1927
46   Wendon, Dublin, 1930
47   Irishtown Library, Dublin, 1932
48   No. 1 Hampstead Avenue, Dublin, 1932
49   Department of Industry and Commerce, Dublin, 1935
50   St Aengus's Church, Co. Donegal, 1967
51   Central Bank, Dublin, 1978
52   The National Gallery of Ireland Millennium Wing, Dublin, 2001
53   The Glucksman Gallery, Cork, 2004
54   Derry City Council Offices, 2005

The failure of the Romans to invade, colonize and develop Ireland, and the consequent failure of the English crown to comprehensively colonize and develop the country after the success of the Norman invasion, are perhaps fundamental to how the architecture of Ireland developed over the last two millennia.

The lack of an early Roman influence meant that for centuries after most other parts of Europe had progressed towards the modern age, the Irish continued as an archaic, cityless but socially complex pastoral society which, although carrying on sporadic trade with its neighbours, was culturally isolated from Europe. Ireland was a heavily forested country, and most buildings were constructed from timber. The coming of Christianity in the fifth century should have brought with it significant influences from the outside world, but while it did bring an element of richness and outward-looking awareness to the culture, the new religion was assimilated and organized on Irish terms rather than those of Rome. Early Christian buildings were of timber construction, and none survives. There are records of stone-built churches from the eighth century on, the earliest buildings being of corbelled construction, either dome-shaped 'beehives' or boat-shaped, as at Gallarus, Co. Kerry. In the ninth century a building type unique to Ireland, the round tower, emerged; although many were destroyed or collapsed, seventy-three are extant.

Ireland continued as an insular and conservative society, protected by its isolation, until the twelfth century, when the powerful influx of European thinking brought by the great colonizing orders, such as the Cistercians and the Augustinians, swiftly followed by the military and political invasion of the Normans, finally opened up the country to outside ideas.

But while Ireland, like all its neighbours, enjoyed a golden age of architecture during the subsequent period of monastery building and landscape development, lack of political unity among the Irish, combined with often shaky rule from England, encouraged the frequent recurrence of rebellions and wars. These were greatly intensified after the sixteenth century by the religious problems arising from the Reformation. Investors tend to avoid prospects where there is political unrest, and so with hardly a few decades of peace at a time between the fifteenth century and the eighteenth century, Ireland became an economic backwater. During brief periods of peace some building took place, building types being confined mainly to ecclesiastical or fortified structures; there are no upstanding examples of the prosperous medieval rural villages that are relatively commonplace in other European countries, because prosperity at that level never evolved.

LEFT
St Aengus's Church, Burt,
Co. Donegal

RIGHT
The Honan Chapel, Cork

Only after the Battle of the Boyne in 1690, with the Dutchman William of Orange on the English throne, did the influences of post-medieval European civilization begin to permeate Ireland. During a period of general peace, safe travel abroad became possible, and travellers brought back to Ireland many progressive ideas in art and architecture. These developments led to another golden age of architecture that began in the mid-1700s and was greatly assisted by the establishment of an Irish parliament in 1784, which allowed the Irish more control over the country's trade and development. The bulk of fine historical architecture to be seen in Ireland today dates from this period, which came to an end in 1800, when the parliament was dissolved and much of the investment in the development of the country was withdrawn as a result.

The nineteenth century was overshadowed by the Great Famine of the 1840s. One third of the 8 million Irish were completely dependent on the potato as their main food source, and when blight caused a series of crop failures between 1845 and 1849 the population was decimated. Many died from starvation and disease, and by 1851 the population had fallen by 1.5 million. The ensuing widespread unrest lasted for decades, and although much was achieved through political and social efforts to improve the lot of the Irish peasant by the end of the century, statistics show that in 1890 70 per cent of the Irish population still lived in mud-walled cottages with sod roofs. For this reason, apart from some village developments, there are very few examples of good secular rural architecture to be found between the great house and the hovel.

The Great Famine failed to have a major effect on urban economy and progress, and although Dublin contained some of the worst slums in Europe it also boasted some fine urban architecture. Among the educated and better off, the Famine further encouraged what was by then a growing awareness of nationhood, and a search for a national culture through art and literature. By the last quarter of the nineteenth century this fresh artistic thinking had led to the creation in architecture of a new Hiberno-Romanesque style, which was followed by a series of rich but ephemeral styles such as Hiberno-Gothic and Celtic Revival, all influenced by the European Arts and Crafts movement.

The new and considerable enthusiasm born of the establishment of the Free State in 1922 gave brief but strong encouragement to the emerging International style, but little architectural development occurred during the Depression of the 1930s. The Second World War was followed by the stagnation of the 1950s and 1960s, when, with very few exceptions, the rigour of architecture in general and the early International style in particular was lost. By the end of the 1960s, though, forward-looking political thinking in Ireland had sown the seeds of prosperity and a new architectural golden age that was born in the late 1980s and came to full flower in the new millennium.

I hope that the following examples will provide a glimpse of how the evolution of the Irish doorway followed that of its architecture.

OPPOSITE
King's Square, Mitchelstown,
Co. Cork

RIGHT
University Church,
St Stephen's Green, Dublin

This stone cairn on the 621-metre summit of Seefin, one of the foothills of the Wicklow Mountains, was constructed in the middle Neolithic period and is similar to many that crown the tops of the north Wicklow range. The landscape of Ireland's east coast was heavily wooded at the time, but on high ground tree cover was thinner and it was easier to clear the land for agriculture. The mantle of peat that covers the mountains today has been in place for 3,000 years, but samples taken from under the peat near Seefin suggest that there was once grazing and crop growing here, before the peat mantle began to grow. It seems reasonable to suppose that the people who worked the land lived in dwellings gathered around the cairn, as the buildings of a medieval village might surround a church.

From the north side of the 26-metre-diameter cairn a narrow low passage, orientated towards the rising sun on midsummer's day, leads to a burial chamber which once contained decorated clay pots filled with the ashes of the people's ancestors. The doorway to the passage consists of two slender posts capped by a lintel slab, all of local granite. Although these elements are rough, undressed stones, they were clearly carefully selected and placed to impart an elegant dignity to the portal. The space between the posts allowed plenty of room for the average person of the Neolithic period to enter, but in the twenty-first century only children and slim adults can do so without difficulty. The passage is roofed and walled with granite slabs, two of which display carved, lozenge-shaped decorations; these are the only such carved stones in the Wicklow group, making this 5,000-year-old tomb unique. A severe earth tremor in the early eighteenth century caused the roof of the chamber to collapse, exposing it to the sky and providing an alternative way to enter this special place.

LEFT AND ABOVE
Cairn at Seefin, Co. Wicklow

the grianan of aileach
inishowen, co. donegal. c.100

While the precise purpose and origins of the prehistoric circular drystone-walled forts or cashels of Ireland are lost in the past, this one, perched on a hilltop on the Inishowen peninsula of Donegal, not only has a wealth of legends relating to it but figures prominently in the historical annals of the region during the first millennium and later. Stone forts of this scale seem to have been used for the holding of ceremonies, as symbols of the power of the local chief and as military fortifications; and the Grianan, sited on Carrowmore Hill at 250 metres above sea level, overlooking and dominating the narrow neck of land connecting the Inishowen peninsula to the mainland, is a fine

example of the type. The 25-metre-diameter structure, dating from the very early Christian period and standing in the centre of earthworks that may date back to the Bronze Age, was the ceremonial headquarters and an important gathering place of the Ui Neills, the northern Gaelic lords.

The only significant feature of the 5.5-metre-high stone façade is the entrance to the fort, an opening facing north-east,

LEFT AND ABOVE
The Grianan of Aileach,
Inishowen, Co. Donegal

14

just over a metre wide and two high, with inclined jambs and a stone lintel over. It is the only entrance and exit from the fort, although legends claim that there is also a secret underground tunnel which connected the chief's quarters to a secluded opening somewhere on the hillside. The massiveness of the great structure says all that is needed about the power of the proprietors; and the small scale of the doorway, which was probably originally closed off by a door made up of thick slabs of oak, accentuates the size of the structure. The doorway leads into a 5-metre-long low, narrow dark passageway which emphasizes the drama of arrival into the brightness of the great inner cirque, and it would have been clear to attackers that even if they managed to breach the door, entering the passageway would be suicidal.

gallarus oratory, dingle, co. kerry, c.8th century

This tiny oratory, measuring 7 metres by 5 metres, perched on rising ground overlooking Ballinskelligs Bay, is a unique survivor of the early Christian corbelled stone form of construction. While a good number of circular corbelled hermitages and oratories, intact and ruined, can be found, particularly in the south-west of Ireland, this more structurally challenging rectilinear form is much rarer. Although there is evidence that the building, built of local old red sandstone, was plastered or pointed internally, no mortar was used in the construction of the masonry. The stones in the 1.2-metre-thick walls were laid with a slight tilt towards the exterior which ensured that the driving rain of many centuries of west Kerry winters never entered the

LEFT AND RIGHT
Gallarus Oratory, Dingle,
Co. Kerry

structure. The geometry of the building has a subtle assymetry that enhances it, and it is possible that it originally had a decorative ridge, pinnacled with carved stone crosses at each end. At the east end is a tiny window that threw morning light on the missal the priest used to celebrate the Eucharist; the arched form of this window suggests that the building was not constructed before the late eighth century.

The simple but dignified doorway is set into the batter of the gable wall, with inclined jambs built of dressed stones spanned by a slender lintel, and the tapering of the 700mm width at ground level to 525mm at the head accentuates the experience of entry or penetration into the inner space. The door, long absent, was probably made from timber: the two pierced stone pintels from which it hung can be seen on the inside face of the wall.

aghowle church, co. wicklow, 9th century

The ruined church at Aghowle is located in an isolated part of County Wicklow on a site that was very important in early Christian times. St Finian established a monastery here in the first quarter of the sixth century, and he is said to have lived at Aghowle for sixteen years, before he moved on and founded the more famous monastery of Clonard in County Meath. Legend tells how St Finian had erected a wonderful bell at Aghowle, the peals of which could be heard for many miles around, and which was much loved by the monastic community there. When he established Clonard, Finian had the bell moved to the new monastery, but it disappeared one night and the following morning was tolling at Aghowle. After a series of unsuccessful attempts to relocate the stubborn bell, Finian gave up and left it in its original home. The church, dating from the eleventh century, is 18.5 metres long by 7.4 metres wide,

and with walls nearly a metre thick and massive, steep gables more than 11 metres high it was clearly an impressive building in its day.

The doorway is of trabeate construction of quartzitic granite, with slightly inclined jambs. While stone arch technology was available at the time, this rather primitive form of doorway, narrow and low, and using great blocks of stone, was used instead to dramatize entry through the considerable thickness of the wall into the church. The location of a bolt hole in the reveal suggests that the original door was nearly 90mm thick, probably made from solid planks of timber and locked in place with a large, square wooden bolt. Most early trabeate doorways were simple and undecorated but that at Aghowle is ornamented by a finely carved architrave in the form of a round moulding decorated with tiny carved stone beading.

OPPOSITE AND BELOW
Aghowle Church, Co. Wicklow

teampull mhuire
glendalough, co. wicklow, 10th century

Deep in the Wicklow Mountains, and about 100 metres outside the main enclosure of the early Christian monastic city of Glendalough, the ruins of Teampull Mhuire stand on a raised earthen platform. Also known as Our Lady's Church and the Woman's Church, the remains consist of a simple, roofless, late-tenth-century nave, built, it is said, on the foundations of an earlier establishment, with a chancel extension that probably dates to the mid-twelfth century. Among the seven churches of Glendalough, this one, standing isolated in a grove of thorn trees, is often missed by visitors because of its secluded location. The church's various names and its location outside the main monastic enclosure suggest that it could have been an establishment for nuns: similar arrangements can be found at other monastic sites in Ireland. A local tradition suggests that this is the site of the burial place of St Kevin, who founded the monastery at Glendalough, and the church was centre of the Patron Day devotions that were held every year on 3 June, the saint's day, until they were discontinued in the nineteenth century because of unruly behaviour and faction-fighting.

The doorway of Teampull Mhuire is constructed from seven large blocks of carved granite that extend through the metre-thick wall. The blocks are decorated externally with a simple raised architrave and the jambs are inclined in the manner that was the style of the time. The great lintel is inscribed on its underside with a saltire or diagonal cross, with circles at the centre and the extremities of the arms: this may be a symbol to denote a place of sanctuary, meaning that a refugee who passes inside may not be pursued or harmed. In the summer of 1825 Sir Walter Scott visited Glendalough, and is said to have sat before this doorway 'lost in admiration at its massive and ancient character'.

LEFT AND RIGHT
Teampull Mhuire,
Glendalough, Co. Wicklow

st cronan's church
tuamgraney, co. clare, 10th century

A monastery was founded on this site by St Cronan in the sixth century and it became a noted place of learning. It was plundered by Vikings in 886 and again in 949, and the present church was probably built by the Abbot Cormac Ua Cillin some time after the latter attack. It consists of the tenth-century western part, which has *antae*, the eastern section, which is a large chancel built in the twelfth century, and a bell tower, erected in the nineteenth century. St Cronan's Church is said to be the oldest church in continuous use not only in Ireland but also in England, Scotland, Wales and France. The east window is a rare example in Ireland of stained glass crafted by the English artist A.E. Childe.

The doorway is a simple and undecorated trabeate opening in the thick gable wall with inclined jambs, typical of its time.

Careful observation will, however, reveal a subtlety: the rough stones that form the jambs and lintel have been cut back to allow a generous architrave to project 20mm beyond the face of the wall. There is no evidence that a solid door hung in the opening: often in a monastic setting when security was not an issue, a sheet of leather was hung instead to keep out the wind. Simple as this door appears, the legendary Brian Boru, the most famous of Ireland's High Kings, is recorded as having passed through it. He provided for ongoing repairs to the church and the round tower that once stood near it, and is recorded as having visited the monastery at least six times. He was killed in the Battle of Clontarf in 1014.

OPPOSITE AND LEFT
St Cronan's Church,
Tuamgraney, Co. Clare

23

The round tower is a building type that is uniquely Irish, and has become a symbol of the Island of Saints and Scholars, as Ireland was described in the Middle Ages. Referred to in the ancient annals as a *cloigteach*, or bell house, a round tower also served as an almost impregnable safe repository for valuable books and monastic relics in times of attack. The wealth of monasteries made them an attractive target for the Vikings, and the power they wielded encouraged sacking by neighbouring Gaelic kingdoms. On warning of an attack, valuables were taken into the tower, to which the only entry was by a sturdy door in an opening a considerable height from the ground. The ladder used for entry would be drawn up into the tower and all the monks had to do was to wait for rescue by the local chieftain. In some cases attackers built large fires under the doorway: in 1097 the tower at Monasterboice was successfully breached, but the books and other valuables of the monastery, together with the monks who guarded them, were consumed by flames.

The round tower at Timahoe was a later addition to the monastery founded here by St Mochua in the seventh century, and it is one of the few such towers to have a doorway richly decorated in the Romanesque style. The doorway is 4 metres from the ground, and the 1.5-metre thickness of the walls is used to create an entrance of dramatic depth, reached by a flight of three steps, each one the base for a Romanesque order of pilasters, of which the two outer ones have carved heads on their capitals. Unusually, there are also carved heads at the base of two of the pilasters. The door opening itself is a little over 1.5 metres high by 50 centimetres wide; it is easy to imagine how difficult it would have been to gain entry if the occupants were defending robustly. Usually the doors to round towers are simple and functional, but in this case it is thought that sacred relics were on occasion put in the doorway on display to the local populace and that it was designed with this ceremonial exposition in mind. On axis with the round tower is a fine piece of sculpture in bronze, granite and limestone by Vincent Browne, depicting a cock, a mouse and a fly placed on a book, illustrating a legend told about St Mochua.

LEFT AND RIGHT
Timahoe Round Tower, Co. Laois

One of the few churches of the Romanesque period that we can date precisely, the Nun's Church is one of a complex of eight churches and two round towers built on the site of one of Ireland's most important early monasteries, founded by St Ciaran in 545. After Ciaran's death, Clonmacnoise – sited in the middle of Ireland where two great cross-country routes, the Shannon River and an ancient road called the Esker Riada, intersect – became a great centre for pilgrimage and scholarship. It was a repository for examples of early Irish art and craftsmanship such as the Cross of Cong and St Kieran's Crozier, but its inland location did not save it from the marauding Vikings, who sailed up the Shannon from Limerick to plunder its riches eight times between 832 and 1164.

Diarmait Mac Murchada, the King of Leinster, coveted Dervorgilla, the wife of Tiernan O'Rourke of Breifne, and abducted her, an action that turned his fellow provincial kings against him and led to his exile. In an attempt to regain his kingdom, he persuaded Henry II of England to provide the assistance of an armed force, and thus began the Norman invasion of Ireland in 1169. In penance for her dalliance with Diarmait, Dervorgilla subsequently became a nun and founded this beautiful little church in a glade of trees outside the main enclosure at Clonmacnoise. Her father, Murchad ó Maelseachlainn, chieftain of Meath, paid for the building, and as befitting the church of a woman of such royalty, the carved stonework is

among the richest of the period. Today, the building is in ruin, but the chancel arch and the doorway hint at its former glory. The featureless façades act as a great foil for the intricately carved doorway, which is set back into the wall in four receding layers or set-backs. Deeply carved chevrons form a major part of the composition, which includes stylized animal heads biting smaller serpents' heads, and more animals with richly decorated heads biting a roll moulding: one of them can be seen gaining a grip on the moulding with its front paws. The doorway enclosed by these decorative jambs is tiny, a mere 85 centimetres wide and 1.65 metres high, its size accentuating the experience of entering the little church.

LEFT, ABOVE AND RIGHT
The Nun's Church,
Clonmacnoise, Co. Offaly

killeshin church, co. laois, 12th century

On the north-east slopes of the Castlecomer plateau a few miles from Carlow town can be found the ruined twelfth-century church of Killeshin. It is all that survives of an important fifth-century Christian monastery founded by St Comgan. Until 1703 there was a round tower near the church, but this is said to have fallen to the ground during a storm in that year. Records state that the strength of the mortar used was such that it lay intact on the ground after its fall.

The doorway to the church, although thought to have been comprehensively rebuilt at some stage, remains one of the most important examples of Romanesque work in Ireland. It consists of four set-back, semi-circular arched rings resting on four receding corner pilasters, the whole surmounted by a steep triangular pediment, a device used over doorways as far back as the late Bronze Age Lion's Gate at Mycenae in Greece. The design of the doorway is in accordance with

'divine proportion' or the Golden Section, a Greek mathematical system setting out the most harmonious division of lines and rectangles. An elaborate inscription in Gaelic on the head of the door, noting the founder of the church, was defaced in the nineteenth century, and atmospheric erosion of the warm, honey-coloured stone over the centuries has reduced the sharpness of the decorative carvings. Enough remains, however, to marvel at, including the rich, interlaced decoration, animals and birds, and a keystone that represents the bearded head of a saint being pecked by two birds. It is very likely that the whole portal was originally painted, with details picked out in bright primary colours.

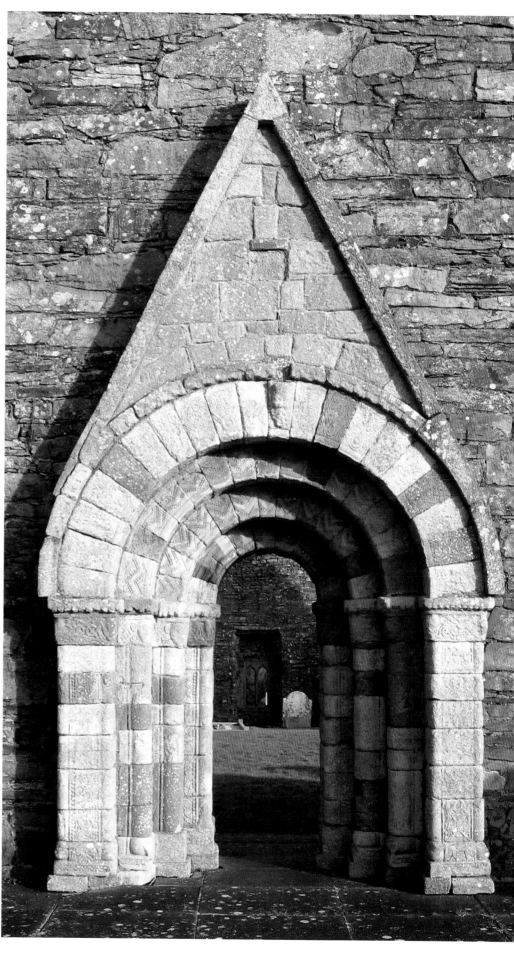

LEFT AND RIGHT
Killeshin Church, Co. Laois

The relative plainness of the main structure of Clonfert Cathedral, which probably dates from the late eleventh century, acts as a perfect foil to the rich and riotously decorated late-twelfth-century doorway that adorns it. The cathedral has undergone many alterations and additions: its early date is indicated by its *antae*. We know the cathedral was burned in the 1170s and rebuilt for a synod that took place in 1179, when the great doorway was probably built. The chancel is of the thirteenth century, while the rather ungainly tower that stands above the west gable, which would be more at home on a Franciscan friary, is of the fifteenth century, as are the lancet windows that flank the doorway.

The mysterious asymmetrical positioning of the doorway in the façade of the gable further accentuates the power of this magnificent doorway, which is perhaps the finest example of a Romanesque doorway in Ireland. The design is an amalgam of many different motifs, but there is a marked absence of the chevron decoration that appears in many Irish examples; the use of heads could indicate French influence, while the triangular diaperwork could be Spanish or English in origin. The narrow door is set back six layers from the façade into the thick wall, its semi-engaged columns supporting a series of arches richly decorated with animal heads, disks and bosses. Rising high above all this is a triangular pediment, the bottom of which has an arcade with five heads which may well originally have had bodies attached. Above this is a triangular pattern of diaperwork with more heads. Every inch of the stonework is carved with intricate interlacing and plants. To truly appreciate the whole composition, you must imagine the building whitewashed, and all the details of the stone-carved decoration sharp, crisp and colourfully painted – something strange to our modern taste.

LEFT AND RIGHT
Clonfert Cathedral,
Co. Galway

31

In the middle of an isolated rural graveyard overlooking the Atlantic coast of Galway stand the ruins of Drumacoo Church, on the site of an early monastic settlement, which may have included a nunnery: the obscure St Sourney is venerated here through a holy well, as she is also on the offshore Aran Islands. It is recorded that near the monastery at the time there was a guest house and a leper house. Early in the thirteenth century the church that stood here then was partially dismantled, rebuilt and extended. It fell into ruin in the seventeenth century, and around 1830 the ruins were extended to create a mausoleum for the St George family of nearby Stradbally, said to be descendants of Baldwin St George, one of William the Conqueror's knights.

There are two entrances to Drumacoo Church: a low and narrow trabeate doorway in the west gable, as was traditional in the pre-twelfth-century period, and the subject of my attention, the thirteenth-century doorway set in the south wall. This fine doorway is particularly interesting as an example of the point of transition from the short-lived, richly Romanesque style of the mid- to late twelfth century to the pointed, linear Gothic style that took over from it. It seems likely that the work here was carried out by a group of stonemasons known to historians as the School of the West, who were active in the late twelfth and early thirteenth centuries in this region, and whose work is characterized by precise joints and rich carving. Here the craftsmen, experts at carving Romanesque decoration, tried out the 'new' Gothic arch, but decorated it in the older style; the result was in what is today called the Transitional style. Two of the arch layers or set-backs are decorated with chevron ornament: the outer one with a moulding strung with filigree-like undercut chevrons, and the inner one with chevrons wrapping a series of pyramids. The jambs are decorated by slender paired shafts with bands, surmounted by a series of richly carved capitals depicting intricately interlaced cats, owls and leaves, the whole truly a proper farewell to the Romanesque.

BELOW AND RIGHT
Drumacoo Church,
Co. Galway

the priory of st edmund
athassel, co. tipperary, c.1260

Built by William de Burgo and confirmed by King John in 1205, the extensive and wealthy Augustinian Priory of St Edmund, at Athassel on the banks of the River Suir, covered much more than the 1.5 hectares of ruins that remain today. Its wealth, however, eventually brought about its destruction. The town that grew up around it was sacked and burned by followers of the Earl of Desmond in 1319, and again by the O'Briens in 1330, and nothing remains of it today: much of the priory itself was destroyed in 1447. What remains is very impressive, though, even in its ruined state. The site was originally an island in the river, and access today is still by the original stone bridge and substantial gatehouse. The remains of the domestic buildings are considerable and include a *necessarium*, that wonderful monastic word for a latrine, but the most significant part of the ruins is the great 65-metre-long cruciform church.

The doorway I have chosen here is not the entrance to the building but the entrance doorway from the nave of the church into the choir, under what must have been a massive crossing tower. It is in the style that is called late Transitional, which generally describes the Gothic arch form where decoration of the stonework is minimized. Under a hood moulding that terminates in two heads are three layers or set-backs. The column capitals carved with floral designs support three arches: the centre arch is plain, while the outer two are carved with chevrons of the Romanesque, so much miniaturized, reduced in depth and filigreed that they hardly resemble chevrons at all.

BELOW AND RIGHT
The Priory of St Edmund,
Athassel, Co. Tipperary

Rosserk Abbey was founded by the Franciscans for the Third Order on a wonderful site overlooking the sand-dune-fringed estuary of the River Moy. The remains are considerable and in a very good state of preservation, a tribute to the stonemasons who constructed them nearly six hundred Mayo winters ago. Third Order Franciscans were allowed to marry and live at home, and this is the only surviving Third Order establishment in Ireland. Local stories tell of the friars here at Rosserk becoming too independent and not taking directions from their superiors; the schism was so bad that the order was forced to abandon the friary to the recalcitrant friars and build a new monastery 5 kilometres to the north at Moyne. The abbey was burned in 1590 by Sir Richard Bingham, the English Governor of Connaught, during a monastic burning spree that also included Moyne Friary and, a little further away, Rathfran Dominican Friary, which had been founded in the thirteenth century.

The doorway, which was originally set in a rendered and probably whitewashed wall, is a Gothic arch finely carved in limestone with an architrave of two pairs of receding mouldings, surmounted by another pair of similar mouldings in the form of an ogee-arched hood with crockets topped with a carved pinnacle. Pilaster finials springing from the arch haunches, which would normally have been decorated with crockets, remain unfinished – mysteriously so, since the fine stone carving in Rosserk seems to be the work of a particularly accomplished mason. Maybe he ran out of time because he had spent so much of it carving little humorous comments, such as the tiny angel with spread wings supporting one of the pointed corbels of the battlemented tower, or the depiction of a round tower – the only such early example – on one of the columns of the sedelia. The ogee arch is thought to have oriental origins, and was certainly widely used structurally in India. It became common in France and England in the fourteenth century, although in England it was mainly used decoratively. The style took nearly another century to make its way to the farthest reaches of Europe and this isolated Franciscan monastery.

BELOW AND RIGHT
Rosserk Abbey, Co. Mayo

the priory of st mary
clontuskert, co. galway, c.1471

An early monastery was founded on this callow site near the River Suck in the eighth century, but much of the buildings surviving today dates back to the mid-twelfth century, when the Arrosian Priory of St Mary was founded here by the powerful O'Kelly clan, who continued to be connected to the place in one way or another for the next four hundred years. The priory and its occupants had a turbulent history. In 1390 the prior was banished by the local bishop, and a few years later the church burned down and had to be rebuilt. A short time after that, one of the priors was killed in battle and in 1463 a canon received a papal absolution for a murder he had committed.

The west doorway, built in 1471, is richly adorned with a compendium of carved stone ornamental features which are probably the finest of their kind in Ireland. The opening is formed by a series of limestone mouldings forming a Gothic arch with an almost indiscernible point. Above the arch and between the two finials that spring from its hood moulding is a decorative carved panel displaying the figures of St Michael, John the Baptist, St Catherine and an unknown bishop, all worth examining in detail. The winged St Michael is a most elaborate figure, with curled hair framing a smiling face. He bears a sword and the scales of justice. On one side of the scales is a soul being attacked by a devil, and on the other side is another devil. The centrepiece of the panel is a stylized tree which grows from vine-leaf foliage that terminates on either side of the panel with two angels, one of which carries a shield bearing a hammer, two dice and a pincer, symbols of the Crucifixion. On either side of the doorway there are exquisite carvings of subjects that include a mermaid with a comb and a mirror, a rose and two animals, probably a griffon and a lion. The figures of the saints and the bishop in particular are placed over the entrance as a banner or statement of those favoured by the priory and as a devotional focus for the local peasants, who were not allowed to enter the church but would have gathered in prayer outside.

LEFT, ABOVE AND RIGHT
The Priory of St Mary,
Clontuskert, Co. Galway

Today a tiny village, Lorrha was once one of the major ecclesiastical centres of the province of Munster, visited by important early saints such as St Patrick and St Brendan. A monastery was founded here by the sixth-century St Ruadhan, and later in medieval times an Augustinian priory and a Dominican friary were established. The ancient manuscript called the Stowe Missal (so called because it was rediscovered in the Duke of Buckingham's library at Stowe House) was probably written here, and Lorrha was also famed as the place where a sacred food-giving tree and the head of St Ruadhan, encased in a silver box, could be viewed. The Protestant churchyard to the east of the village is the site of the monastery founded by St Ruadhan, as well as the scant remains of two very early high crosses and the nineteenth-century parish church. Next to it are the roofless ruins of a thirteenth-century church, which has an interesting door.

The ruined structure has *antae*, which suggests that it was built pre-1000, and we know from the annals that it was rebuilt in the thirteenth century after partial destruction during local wars. It was altered again in the fifteenth century, at which time a new doorway was inserted into the thirteenth-century one. The older doorway consists of a simple hooded Gothic arch in

limestone, originally supported on slender columns. The capitals of these have some restrained ornament: the only embellishment is the head of a smiling saint, probably Ruadhan, at the point of the arch. The later doorway has a rich range of typically fifteenth-century carved ivy leaves and flowers, each of which may once have had a meaning that is now lost in the past. There is also a representation of a pelican, no doubt by a stonemason who had never seen one: often depicted feeding its own blood to its young, the pelican is a powerful symbol of charity in Christian art. The width between the jambs of the doorway suggests that there was originally another, inner arch.

ABOVE AND RIGHT
Lorrha, Co. Tipperary

rathborney church
near ballyvaughan, co. clare, c.1500

The medieval parish church of Rathborney lies within a large earthbanked enclosure, presumably the 'rath' in the name. Although much of the upstanding walls and the doorway date to the early sixteenth century, parts of the stonework are a couple of centuries earlier, and the existence of the rath suggests that the original structure here may go back to early Christian times. The east window, made up of four separate slender cusp-arched opes, is a particularly fine example of decorative Gothic stonework. The moss-covered bullaun stone that can be found 10 metres from the church door is additional evidence of the antiquity of the site, and suggests that it may have been a cere-monial centre long before Christianity came to these parts.

The doorway of generous width, set in the south wall one-quarter of the way along its length, is a round Gothic form in cut limestone. The lower jambs are missing, but the arch, including an elaborate hood moulding, is decorated with thirteen separate convex and angled layers or set-backs of stone. They are all almost as sharp as the day they were carved and, together with the fine windows, are evidence that a school of master masons was then at work in this part of County Clare. A part of the process of entering and exiting holy places at the time – a custom that has continued to the present day – was the anointing of oneself by making the sign of the Cross with blessed water, often from a holy well source, for which purpose here an elaborate holy water stoup with a miniature, vaulted ceiling is built into the thickness of the wall in the right jamb of the doorway.

LEFT
Rathborney Church and the bullaun stone

RIGHT
Detail of doorway

carrick castle, carrick-on-suir, co. tipperary, c.1565

Sited beside a fifteenth-century tower house on the banks of the River Suir, this Tudor manor house, of a type relatively common in England and particularly in the Cotswolds, is for Ireland a unique survival. It was built by Black Tom, the 10th Earl of Ormond, related through Anne Boleyn to Elizabeth I, and whom she called her 'Black Husband'. He was reared in the English court until he was twenty-two, and would have been familiar with the finest English architecture of the time; it is said that he built the manor house to attract Elizabeth to visit him in Ireland. A favourite summer residence of the 12th Earl and Great Duke of Ormond in the seventeenth century, it survived into the twentieth century when, in a state of dilapidation, it was rescued by the Office of Public Works.

Although at first glance the entrance at Carrick Castle consists of a simple doorway, its context and detailing are quite sophisticated. Similar to the doorways of the common tower house, it takes the form of a chamfered limestone round arch, but it is more generous in width and covered with a cut-stone hood moulding. Its importance is particularly emphasized by its setting in a breakfront with a generous six-light oriel window topped by a finial-topped gable and two-light attic window above parapet level. The breakfront has a pronounced batter that springs from below the terminals of the hood moulding; the batter has the effect of broadening the chamfer of the arch to where it ends neatly above ground level in an angled block. The pair of doors, hung from iron hinges behind a rebate in the stonework, are recent: the original would probably have been made from broad planks studded to horizontal rails behind, and the joints protected by moulded cover strips.

OPPOSITE AND BELOW
Carrick Castle,
Carrick-on-Suir,
Co. Tipperary

shee alms house, rose street, kilkenny, 1582

Late-medieval urban buildings are rare in Ireland, but some survivors can be found in the towns of Galway and Kilkenny. The wealthy and influential Shee family owned a number of properties in Kilkenny in the sixteenth century, two of which were unfortunately demolished relatively recently. That at Rose Street, built by Sir Richard Shee, a distinguished lawyer, and his wife for the accommodation of twelve poor citizens of Kilkenny, survived, however, as a charitable institution until the late nineteenth century. Three of the windows and the carved plaque on the right are later insertions, and but for the other plaque, which displays the arms of Richard Shee, the façade with its three hood mouldings and the simple central doorway portrays a calm symmetry. The building was rescued by Kilkenny Corporation in the 1980s and is now open as a tourist office.

The modest Gothic doorway is formed from twelve blocks of carved limestone with a generous chamfer that terminates 30cm above street level. While the stones of the jamb are quite roughly formed, even the damage and erosion of over 400 years fail to disguise the more finely worked arrises of the stones of the arch. The official cast-iron Ancient Monuments plaque above the door describing the building, and the one higher up announcing the Corporation's intervention, tend to disfigure the doorway and the façade. The door is recent: the original would probably have been vertically planked and fixed with iron studs to horizontal battens at the back.

LEFT AND RIGHT
Shee Alms House, Rose
Street, Kilkenny

49

portumna castle, portumna, co. galway, c.1618

A unique castle in the Irish context, Portumna Castle was an unusually advanced and radical design for its day, displaying architectural thinking that might easily be regarded as belonging to the eighteenth or nineteenth century. It was erected by Richard Burke, 4th Earl of Clanricard, and his wife, Frances Walsingham. She was the widow of Robert Devereaux, for five months in 1599 Lord Lieutenant of Ireland, before he was executed for treason. The Burkes were descended from the Norman de Burgos, who originally came to Ireland with Prince John on his wild-oats-sowing, tearaway tour of 1185. The 4th Earl is said never to have spent a night in his castle, not an uncommon occurrence in those days, reflecting the enormous wealth of English landowners and their absentee habits. Subsequent descendants did, however, live in the place and in spite of a number of sieges it was occupied continually by the Burkes until it was accidentally burnt down in 1828. It has recently been refurbished by the state.

The advanced nature of the design of the castle goes further than the plan arrangement: the approach and entrance to the castle is conceived on a sophisticated and formal axial basis. The main gates to the castle open on to a long gravel driveway that leads through three courtyards and two elaborate interim portals to the entrance, with the full splendour of the building gradually being revealed. At the third gateway, a pinnacled Renaissance-inspired concoction displaying the arms of the Clanricard family, visitors would dismount from their horses or carriages and proceed on foot through the third garden to the entrance to the castle.

The castle doorway is a fine and scarce example of quality secular architecture of the time. Reached by a staircase with elegantly curved balustrades, an eighteenth-century addition, the doorway, a cut-limestone arch within a simple rectilinear frame, is topped by a richly decorative pediment of pinnacles and stylized eagles and a central glazed oval that doubled as a gun port. Further evidence of the turbulent nature of the early seventeenth century can be seen in the gun loops placed on both sides of the doorway in which to position guns to greet unwelcome visitors.

LEFT AND RIGHT
Portumna Castle, Portumna, Co. Galway

southwell gift houses, kinsale, co. cork, 1682

Apart from caring for the sick, medieval religious monasteries also provided accommodation for those in society who were unable to work because of age or disability. Some time after the monasteries were abolished in the sixteenth century it became fashionable for local overlords to provide and maintain almshouses for favoured tenants who had grown too old to work. They were usually built in a terrace on a street or as a cluster around a common court, much as sheltered housing is today. Because they were being provided by the lord of the manor, they were, although modest in scale, usually built by the manorial craftsmen using the best materials. England is particularly rich in such almshouses, but there are a few surviving examples in Ireland, the earliest of which, built in 1634, can be found at Youghal in County Cork. The Southwell family of Gloucester in England owned estates in County Cork and County Limerick from the time of Charles I and over the years were involved in charitable works in Kinsale; these included the provision of a little complex of almshouses called the Southwell Gift Houses, built to cater for eight widows of 'decayed' Protestant tradesmen. The eight cottages are arranged on two sides of a richly planted garden, and over-looked by a two-storey Master's House.

LEFT AND RIGHT
Southwell Gift Houses,
Kinsale, Co. Cork

The Master's House is particularly imposing relative to the modest widows' apartments: it is raised high above them and the garden and is reached by a flight of twelve stone steps. It is the unusual doorway, however, a unique and elaborate concoction of classical elements contrived in brick, which draws the eye. It consists of a shallow porch built from red brick that projects less than a metre from the plain plastered façade, and is as much an announcement as an entrance: a large brick-framed stone plaque over the door displays the complex coat of arms of the Southwells and the date 1682. Brick had limited use in Ireland until the mid-seventeenth century, but here it is used in an extraordinarily plastic way, a tour de force of classical pilasters, capitals, corbels and cappings.

In the last quarter of the seventeenth century, after decades of wars, there were large numbers of soldiers in the army who were elderly and infirm, prompting one reporter to remark that when on the march the army 'are forc't to hire carts to carry the old and Decayed men'. Owing in part to the need for good public relations when recruiting, the erection of retirement homes to provide care for veterans and disabled soldiers had become common in Europe in the early seventeenth century. The Duke of Ormond, who became Viceroy of Ireland in 1677, established Ireland's first hospital to cater for army veterans to the west of the city of Dublin, and laid the foundation stone in 1680. The result is Ireland's first large building in the classical style, of such a scale and grandeur that, initially, it must have been viewed with astonishment by the citizens of Dublin, and the three hundred veterans whom it accommodated.

The building is planned as four sides of an almost square courtyard, and each side has an entrance. The principal entrance is on the north front, overlooking the River Liffey and beyond it the Phoenix Park, and consists of a doorway with a round arch enclosing a delicately carved Portland stone tympanum. Framing it is a segmental pediment supported on Corinthian pilasters, above which, in the most important position on the façade of the building, where one might normally find a royal coat of arms, are the large and flamboyant arms of the Duke of Ormond. Finely carved in limestone, they clearly stamp his ownership on the idea and the building. Soaring above is the clock tower and spire, completed in the early years of the 1700s.

LEFT AND RIGHT
The Royal Hospital, Kilmainham,
Dublin

beaulieu, drogheda, co. louth, c.1700

The estate of Beaulieu, on the north banks of the River Boyne east of the town of Drogheda, has existed for 800 years, and in all that time has changed hands only once. The Plunkett family established the estate after the Norman invasion, and remained in residence here until the mid-seventeenth century, when the estate was forfeited because of William Plunkett's involvement in the rebellion of 1641. The Plunketts were replaced by Sir Henry Tichborne, who was living there from 1650, and who became Marshal of the Irish Army when Charles II was restored to power in 1660. His son came into the ownership of the Beaulieu estate by the Act of Settlement in 1662. The house that we see today is probably the result of major alterations and remodelling carried out to the original Plunkett manor house around 1700 by Henry Tichborne, Sir Henry's grandson. A well-proportioned seven-bay structure with a steeply pitched and impressively cantilevered hipped, slated roof, it is a blend of Williamite and classical influences, a style not common in the larger houses of Ireland at the time.

There is no coy delaying of the moment of arrival at this house by a meandering avenue: a 100-metre driveway leads straight from the entrance gates to the front door, allowing approaching visitors plenty of time to admire the proportions, colour and solidity of the house. The doorway is the most elaborate and largest element of the elevation that faces the visitor: it almost crowds out the windows above and on either side. A flight of limestone steps leads to an elegant doorcase that is a blend of warm brick and pale limestone. The doorcase is flanked by two brick pilasters with carved limestone Corinthian capitals supporting a brick segmental pediment, lightened by delicate limestone dentils, framing a swagged limestone ornament. The double doors, hung in a carved hardwood frame, are probably those originally fitted, a series of hardwood planks fixed with diamond-shaped iron studs, the joints between the planks covered with rounded mouldings, giving a pleasing sophisticated finish.

BELOW AND RIGHT
Beaulieu, Drogheda, Co. Louth

56

dr steevens's hospital, dublin, 1733

When Dr Richard Steevens, a Dublin physician, Fellow of the Royal College of Physicians and Professor of Physics at Trinity College, died in 1710 at the age of fifty-six, he left a legacy to his twin sister Grizel that was to be expended, after her death, on the construction of a modern hospital in Dublin. His sister, however, wanted the hospital to be built in her lifetime, so in 1717 she appointed a board of trustees to make the arrangements and seek the additional funding that was necessary for the work. Thomas Burgh, Surveyor of Works and Fortifications and architect of the old library building at Trinity College, Dublin, prepared plans for the building, and it was finally completed in 1733 under the supervision of the English architect Edward Lovett Pearce, who succeeded Burgh. It was the first 'modern' hospital to be built in Ireland.

The main entrance to the building is on the east side, facing narrow Steevens's Lane, but in 1987 the building was radically refurbished and converted for use as a Health Board office. As part of that work, a range of nineteenth-century buildings to the north was demolished to make way for an entrance court, and a new main entrance doorway, a copy of the original, was located on the north elevation. The original doorway is a robust and heavy early Georgian design, with a sharply detailed

LEFT AND RIGHT
Dr Steevens's Hospital, Dublin

RICARDUS STEEVENS M.D. DOTAVIT
GRISELL STEEVENS SOROR EIUS EDIFICAVIT

An° Dn̄i
1720

segmental pediment supported on two pilasters with extended capitals, within which the doorway is framed by an elliptical arch. Four steps lead to the door, which is made from sheet iron with decorative strapwork, over which there is an open fanlight with a fine wrought-iron design. A plaque over the doorway proclaims the names Richard and Grizel Steevens in Latin and the date 1720, when the work commenced. It is not an entrance to inspire calm and restfulness to the legions of patients who were brought in here during the hospital's history, and could just as easily be the doorway to a jail. Only the bubbled iron doors and the venerable state of the old limestone, leeching warm pink tones of long-latent minerals, give it today a harmless aura.

Knock Abbey today consists of a squat fourteenth-century tower house, built by the Bellew family, with much of the stone coming from an abbey that existed on the site in the mid-twelfth century, and extensions that are Elizabethan, Georgian, Victorian and early twentieth century. The Victorian architect William Caldbeck castellated the tower house and built an extension to contain a fine library, but much of the house and library were burned in 1923 by the IRA. The tower house and the Elizabethan and Georgian sections of the building escaped damage, and in 1925 a substantial new section in the castellated Gothic style was built on the south side, to the designs of W.S. Barber. The house and 12 hectares of overgrown gardens were purchased in 1997 by Cyril O'Brien. He set about extensive restoration work, and succeeded in saving many of the ancient and rare trees, which include a tulip tree that probably dates from the late seventeenth century. The gardens are open to the public from May to September.

The doorway in the tower house was probably inserted during the Georgian period; this was early for such a strong Gothic form, but it was probably inspired by the abbey that originally occupied the site. The intricate Gothic framing of the fanlight over the glazed panel doors is a pleasant relief from the sober and rather dull elevation of the seven-bay Georgian wing. Somehow, however, and maybe deliberately, the Georgian architect overdid the scale of the receding architrave mouldings of the Gothic stone doorway, and the doorway dominates the strong keep that it decorates, and draws attention to and frames the exquisite delicacy of the doors and the fanlight, which is supported by four clustered columns with acanthus-leaved capitals.

LEFT AND RIGHT
Knock Abbey, or Thomastown
Castle, Co. Louth

king's square
mitchelstown, co. cork, 1780

Mitchelstown was founded as a market town in the thirteenth century, and became the chief residence of the White Knights, through whom it and 40,500 hectares of land eventually passed in the eighteenth century to the Earls of Kingston. A new town was laid out by the 4th Earl of Kingston in 1775, making it one of the earliest planned towns in Ireland, and the excellently proportioned King's Square has survived almost intact. The lower part of the square was built in about 1780, and the upper part was completed in 1820, resulting in one of the finest Georgian squares in Ireland. The lower part, called Kingston College, was never planned as an educational establishment, but was intended as an almshouse providing accommodation for elderly Protestants.

The residents are housed in separate units in a long two-storey terrace, relieved and embellished by the insertion of a five-bay house in the centre and a variety of entrance doors. The terrace is further punctuated by the insertion of two pedimented gable fronts in cut limestone, of almost monumental scale, although fronting ordinary houses. It is clear that the designer had fun with these: in each case two great piers of chamfered ashlar limestone support massive consoles, which in turn support a triangular pediment. Located between these piers is a pair of front doors, each with a generous rectilinear fanlight over it, above which a diocletian window lends a wonderful lightness to the whole.

OPPOSITE AND BELOW
King's Square, Mitchelstown,
Co. Cork

Spectacularly sited on the brink of high cliffs below the rambling and vast ruins of Downhill Castle, Mussenden Temple is a king among teahouses. Designed by Michael Shanahan and built by Frederick Augustus Hervey, Bishop of Derry and Earl of Bristol, it was intended as a Grecian temple in honour of Mrs Frideswide Mussenden, a young woman whose name was linked with that of the 52-year-old bishop at the time of his separation from his wife. Mrs Mussenden died at the age of twenty-two, shortly before the temple was completed. It was used for some years afterwards as a library, but fell into disuse after the bishop's death in 1799. The Latin inscription around the dome is a quotation from Lucretius that the poet Dryden translated as

'Tis pleasant, safely to behold from shore
The rolling ship, and hear the tempest roar.

The doorway has a simple surround surmounted by a flat-topped pediment, and is reached by an elegantly tapering, balustraded stone staircase of thirteen steps. One might expect the entrance to a building of such a scale to be more imposing, but the modest door may be a deliberate effort to magnify the effect of entering and being presented with the tall circular interior and three windows, facing west, north and east. The understated doorway is, however, given strength by the flanking half-engaged Corinthian columns, soaring twice the height of the door, above which is a finely carved plaque in Portland stone bearing the arms of the bishop. A slight shortcoming in the whole is the fact that, although even the over-door pediment takes up the curvature of the temple, the tapering stairs do not.

BELOW AND RIGHT
Mussenden Temple, Co. Derry

63 merrion square, dublin, 1791

In the terraced urban houses of the mid- to late eighteenth century the doorway became the single decorative feature in an otherwise simple brick façade, and towards the end of the century the elements used in its design became more delicate, reflecting, in carved stone, aspects of the fine stuccowork to be found in the interior of the house. Semicircular arches framing fanlights over front doors were introduced in Irish townhouses early in the eighteenth century, and by late in the century brick arched fanlights in excess of 2 metres in diameter were common, throwing into the hallways additional light that gave more emphasis to the decoration of ceilings and walls. The fanlight was a finely crafted element, using slender mullions of timber or a lead and iron alloy in a 'sunburst' or 'peacock' motif. Doorways were placed set back from the street on a platform a

few steps higher than the public pavement, to make a clearly established threshold. The great Georgian squares of Dublin were built in lots of two or three houses over a number of years, often with different heights, widths, colour of bricks and doorcases, creating a whole that remains today rich in unselfconscious variety.

While many of Dublin's Georgian doorcases have been altered over time, with cut stone being painted over and replacement fanlights fitted, that at 63 Merrion Square – apart from having its cast-iron doorknob replaced with a decorative brass one and brass plates added – has changed little since it was built in 1791. The fanlight is made in the form of beaded mullions and swags with decorative rosettes. Below the fanlight a breakfront frieze in limestone is supported by Ionic columns

and pilasters, and decorated with classical grooves and rosettes. Between the capitals of the columns and the pilasters, and above the glazing of the sidelights, another panel displays a large rosette with a beaded and radiating leaf motif surround-ing a rose. The eight-panel door, made from imported pine of high quality, is the original. A fine feature not visible externally is the door lock and latch encased in a large brass-bound mahogany block fixed to the inner face.

ABOVE

Merrion Square, south

RIGHT

63 Merrion Square, Dublin

69

kilmainham gaol, dublin, 1796

When the English preacher and prison reformer John Howard visited the old Kilmainham gaol in 1787, he found many of the inmates roaring drunk before noon on whiskey that had been passed to them through the bars of the windows from the street. His report contributed to the decision to build a new gaol high on Gallows Hill, in the suburbs west of Dublin, and the new building was opened for business in 1796. Before long it was filled to capacity with burglars, pickpockets, rapists, bigamists and counterfeiters, but the most common cause of imprisonment at the time was debt, and over half the inmates were debtors. Within less than 100 years, however, Kilmainham took on a new historic importance, as an increasing number of Irish nationalists found themselves incarcerated there from time to time. There are, indeed, very few prominent figures in the nationalist movement who did not spend time in Kilmainham Gaol: Robert Emmet, leader of the 1803 uprising, Charles Stewart Parnell, leader of the Irish Party, and Eamon de Valera, insurrectionist of 1916 and later President of Ireland, are just three.

The gaol is surrounded by high walls interrupted only at the entrance, which is approached from the street via a small courtyard. The doorway has a macabre feel to it, and no prisoner being brought to it could fail to realize that they were entering a place apart. Set back from the façade of chamfered ashlar granite, the narrow but heavy iron door, fronted by a wrought-iron gate, is set in an intricately carved stone panel of what can only be described as maggot-like rustication. Above the door is a deeply carved tympanum portraying five chained serpent-like dragons, known as the Five Devils of Kilmainham.

LEFT, ABOVE
Kilmainham Gaol and
the Five Devils

LEFT AND RIGHT
Kilmainham Gaol doorway

cove cottage. stradbally, co. waterford. c.1810

Stradbally is a pretty little village on the coast of County Waterford which became popular, in common with other coastal villages of mild climate, as a place of resort in the late eighteenth century. This cottage orné, where the well-off classes could enjoy a rural vacation, was built in the early days of the popularity of 'taking the waters' on the road leading from the village to the sea. Its similarity with the typical Irish thatched cottage starts and ends with the thatch: compared with the tiny mud cabins that were home to most Irish peasants, this is quite a big house, with ample high-ceilinged rooms, large windows, and a central entrance hall.

The entrance to the cottage is a well-considered rustic set piece, and in spite of the small scale there is a sequential process of approach and entrance that would not be unusual in a building of much larger scale. A nine-panelled door topped by a simple spider's web fanlight is reached through a fragrant and polychromatic cottage garden filled with traditional cottage plants. The gateway to be entered first, however, tells us that this is not an ordinary cottage: the two stuccoed gate piers are topped by carved stone cappings sporting a stylized Greek motif called an acroterion at the corners, and between them hangs a finely crafted wrought-iron gate. Inside the gate three steps have to be climbed, further emphasizing the process and ceremony of approach.

LEFT AND RIGHT
Cove Cottage, Stradbally,
Co. Waterford

the king's inns. broadstone. dublin. 1817

Designed in 1800 by the most prominent architect of the period in Ireland, James Gandon, and reported to be among his favourite works, the King's Inns, headquarters of Dublin's barristers, was completed in 1817 by Francis Johnston. It is less well known than Gandon's other great Dublin works, the Custom House and the Four Courts, though unlike them it escaped destruction during the War of Independence and the Civil War. Instead of locating the principal façade to address Henrietta Street, a fine Georgian street to the east of the site, Gandon designed the building to face west towards Constitution Hill over a small park. This elevation has two grand entrances, one leading to the great dining hall and the other originally to the library.

The doorway leading to the dining room is a sculptural part of the overall classical composition of one of the two three-bay breakfronts on this façade. The scale and proportions of the doorway are carefully handled: three steps lead to the entry

level, and inside a flight of nine more accentuate the process of entering. It is a powerful doorway, partly imbued by the two regal but smiling caryatids flanking the opening, offering food and drink, and supporting the classical pediment. The figures represent Ceres, the goddess of plenty, holding a cornucopia, and Bacchante, a female follower of Bacchus, god of wine, holding a goblet of wine. In a war against the Caryea in the Peloponnesus, the Greeks exterminated all the males and reduced the women to slavery. The victory was celebrated thereafter in Greek architecture by using statuary representing the women in a servile stance, supporting entablatures – thus the name *caryatides*. The style was resurrected in a dramatic way in the nineteenth century, although the women were often replaced by Herculean men, as in many mid-to-late-nineteenth-century urban doorways in Central Europe. By contrast, the caryatids flanking the library doorway at the King's Inns are old bearded men holding books and keys.

LEFT AND RIGHT
The King's Inns,
Broadstone, Dublin

bridge house. kilkenny, c.1820

Although known as Bridge House, this structure, sited by a bridge over the River Nore and often featuring in the foreground of photographs of Kilkenny Castle across the river, consists of two adjoining houses. Most of what you see today dates from the late eighteenth century, but the bow-fronted part nearest the river, No. 89 John Street, conceals the remains of structures dating back to a number of centuries earlier, and there is some evidence that it was part of the medieval Norman priory of St John. No. 89 has fine stucco ceilings and fireplace mantles, and with its bow front, one of only two in Kilkenny, it is an excellent example of a house of its period.

The fine double doorcase under a single fanlight is one of two in Kilkenny, the other being in Parliament Street. There is no evidence that Nos 88 and 89 John Street have ever been anything but separate houses, but during alterations in 1820 this unusual doorway was inserted: a thin party wall between the halls of both houses can be seen behind the central mullion of the fanlight. Under a rather flat fanlight arch in limestone, two semi-engaged Tuscan columns support an entablature and frieze decorated with pateras and fluting; the wrought-iron gateway at the street and seven limestone steps up to the doorway give the composition great importance.

LEFT AND RIGHT
Bridge House, Kilkenny

lacy's public house, loan, co. kilkenny, 1825

This little rural building, sited gable on to the road, has a background that reflects aspects of the history of not only the locality but also rural Ireland as a whole. While the oaten straw thatch and ropework ridge are a fine recent restoration, parts of the whitewashed mud walls belong to a building that was used as a Catholic chapel from penal times to the late eighteenth century, when it is said the legendary Father Murphy of Kilcormick in County Wexford, later to be executed for his part in the 1798 rebellion, preached here. After becoming disused as a chapel it probably became a farm dwelling, and in the latter part of the nineteenth century, when agricultural prices were poor, it became a public house. The current owner, whose family have run the pub since early in the twentieth century, has a strong appreciation of the importance of the building as local heritage, and has preserved not only the external appearance but also its traditional interior.

The wonderfully naïve doorway boldly displays the name of the proprietor in raised plaster letters, while most other rural pubs of its period would have had only a discreet plaque claiming it to be licensed to sell alcohol and tobacco. The door, which can be opened complete or in the traditional 'half-door' configuration, is recent but based on the original. The name board is set on the face of a shallow porch projecting from the façade, but the crowning glory of this doorway is the pair of naïve but quite convincing classical fluted pilasters, complete with Ionic capitals, which flank the door and support the canopy.

LEFT, ABOVE AND RIGHT
Lacy's Public House, Loan,
Co. Kilkenny

The Society for Charitable Instruction, later known as the Presentation Sisters, is an order of nuns founded in the city of Cork in 1776 by Nano Nagle, primarily to provide religious and secular education for the poor. The order later spread around the world. The first school in Thurles was set up in an ordinary house in 1817, and very soon it became clear that it could not take all the children who flocked to its doors. With the help of the Liberator, Daniel O'Connell, and Edmund Rice, the founder of the Christian Brothers, funds were gathered and the foundation stone was laid in 1824 for a new convent. The building, which contained living accommodation, a chapel and school rooms, was designed, records state, by 'an architect from London'.

It was and remains today a plain building, but evidence of the involvement of an architect with a strong sense of occasion and style is offered by the design of the main doorway, which, although very secular in feel, must have proved irresistible to the nuns. The plainness of the façade acts as a perfect foil to this exuberant entrance. The door itself, decorated with Gothic motifs, is flanked by two slender Gothic sidelights, but the feature that makes the doorway unique and uplifting is the magnificent cartwheel sunburst fanlight.

LEFT AND RIGHT
Presentation Convent,
Thurles, Co. Tipperary

For as many centuries as the horse has been in Ireland, and up until the middle of the twentieth century, the farrier or smith had an important place in both the rural and urban world. Forges were as common as filling stations in cities and throughout the countryside, and they played an important part in the social as well as the commercial life of every neighbourhood, village and hamlet. The blacksmith's forge was a one-man factory, where not only were horses shod, but ploughshares, billhooks, nails, gates and practically everything iron needed by the community was produced. Forges were usually sited close to a stream or pond, from where the trough, in which red hot metal was quenched, could be easily replenished. The blacksmith, as a tradesman, was usually looked up to and, serving a wide range of people from all classes, he would have been a reliable source of news and information. In Ireland the forge was often a centre of political agitation, and frequently the place where many of the pikes used in the rebellions were made.

Enniskerry is the estate village of Powerscourt House, largely built in the Romantic style by the Wingfields of Powerscourt during the years of the early to mid-nineteenth century. The forge here, which cost £150 to build, is a simple building enlivened with little affectations such as the shouldered *antae* on the gables and the fine-pointed finial, as sharp today as it was when it was carved from local granite. There can be few buildings where the doorway leaves as little doubt about the building's purpose as this forge: the horseshoe-shaped doorway of granite blocks was a style popular at the time for such buildings, and in this case the stonemason has not only included the groove characteristic of iron shoes but articulated the stone 'shoe' with the appropriate nail holes.

LEFT AND RIGHT
Forge at Enniskerry,
Co. Wicklow

first presbyterian church. antrim. 1837

LEFT AND RIGHT
First Presbyterian Church,
Antrim

This church is an example of just one of a rich range of styles that were tested during the period of revivalism that began in the late eighteenth century and lasted into the nineteenth, and of which Gothic Revival was the only real survivor. Built to the designs of John Millar of Belfast, and one of only a few churches for which he was responsible in Northern Ireland before he emigrated to New Zealand, this is a fine and rare example of the Greek Revival style of the time. The uncompromising simplicity of its lines and the paucity of decoration could almost cause it be to mistaken for a work of the recent Post Modern style.

The church is sited 100 metres back from Antrim's Main Street at the end of a paved avenue of ornamental trees, allowing plenty of time for those approaching to admire the entrance façade. Apart from the triangular pediment and the flanking slender triple light windows, the front façade consists mainly of the entrance, which is massive, dramatic and full of ceremony, and takes up almost half of the front façade. Framed by a subtle set-back in the façade and a shallow arch, the entrance doors are flanked by a pair of large and perfectly proportioned Greek Doric columns with recessed bases. Reached by two flights of five and three steps, the 3-metre-high doorway is recessed 2 metres back from the front wall. The doorway opening has inclined jambs that impart an Egyptian monumental quality and contrast well with the rectilinear lines of the rest of the building.

former belfast bank. armagh. 1850

This neatly proportioned building, said to have been designed by Charles Lanyon, is built in a faintly Florentine Baroque style, with a strongly rusticated red sandstone façade and a generous cornice topped by a balustrade. It operated as a bank from 1850 until 1990, when it was acquired by Armagh Council, and it is now part of a visitors' centre. The strong horizontal lines of the cornice are balanced by the verticality of the three arched elements in the façade, the central doorway and the two tall recessed windows, each of which has a carved head keystone.

The doorway has an architrave with egg and dart motif, interrupted on the jambs by ornately carved Gibbsian blocks, surrounding a pair of panel doors with bolection mouldings. The crowning glory of the doorway is the pediment and richly carved tympanum filling the arch above it. At a time when there was considerable competition between the many banks to attract custom by projecting a strong image of probity and solidity, the Belfast Bank Company in this case cheekily used no less than the arms of the City of Belfast to demonstrate its importance in the Victorian world. The arms display emblems that were used by seventeenth-century Belfast merchants on their coinage – a chained wolf and a seahorse, addressing a plaque that includes a white marble panel depicting a three-masted merchant ship – and were intended to convey a strong announcement that those who entered with their money would be in safe hands. It is such a pity that the wonderful crafts-manship of this doorway is spoiled by thoughtless placing of signage and bins.

LEFT AND RIGHT
Former Belfast Bank, Armagh

broadstone station. dublin. 1850

Broadstone Station was designed in the late 1840s by the architect to the Midland Great Western Railway, John Skipton Mulvany, and was completed in 1850. In spite of its current near-dereliction, Broadstone is one of Dublin's most impressive examples of Victorian architecture. The railway age had arrived in Ireland less than thirty years before, and architects employed by the different railway companies had no precedents to inform their designs for the substantial new buildings required, so a quest for a suitable style for an ideal railway architecture ensued. William Deane Butler used an Italianate, towered design for Amiens Street (now Connolly) Station in 1844; Sancton Wood continued the Italian influence in his designs for Kingsbridge (now Heuston) Station in 1845 but concentrated on an Italian Renaissance style. Mulvany consciously sought his inspiration from farther afield, designing for Broadstone a monumental neo-Egyptian structure with classical details that, sited as it is on an eminence, dominates all around it, inspiring Maurice Craig to suggest that a traveller happening upon it 'feels a little as he might if he were to stumble unawares upon the monstrous silences of Karnak or Luxor'.

The doorway, a slender 4-metre-high opening with inclined jambs, is located in the centre of the great south front of the building. The door is set back a metre from the outer structural opening in the façade of a great pylon which, surmounted by a classical pediment decorated by a glorious coved anthemion, bursts through the pediment to dominate it, soaring to finish with a cornice and parapet 2.5 metres above it. Seven steps ascend to the doorway between great granite blocks surmounted by wrought-iron lamps, now broken, but which must have been magnificent in their day. The entrance hallway within is impressive, a three-storey height overlooked by a first-floor gallery supported on Doric columns, pilasters and piers. The unswept landing before the door, protected by a pathetic little railing, and the poor condition of the doors themselves, cannot hide this entrance's grand magnificence.

LEFT AND RIGHT
Broadstone Station, Dublin

ERECTED
A.D.1850

University Church was built by John Henry Newman (1801–90), an English cleric of the Church of England who became a Catholic at the age of forty-four. In 1851 he was appointed Rector of a new Catholic university to be founded in Dublin, which was eventually to become University College, Dublin. In 1855 he had University Church built to the designs of John Hungerford Pollen, who was Professor of Fine Art at the new university. The resulting building has one of the finest nineteenth-century interiors in Dublin. It is a place of Byzantine marbles, mosaics and fine wall paintings, an oasis of peace and beauty in the middle of a busy city.

Originally the entrance to the church was set back from the street and was some 1.5 metres below street level, but in 1856 Newman wrote to Pollen 'please send by return of post if you can a porch'. The result, presumably not by return of post, was this wonderful entrance, creating an exotic presence protruding audaciously on to the street between the comparative drabness of a classical cut-limestone façade and a typical mid-eighteenth-century brick house. Four tiny limestone Byzantine columns on large bases, with capitals decorated with stylized motifs of each of the four evangelists, are arranged in two pairs supporting a deep double arch of thin bricks. Set well back under the upper arch is a shallow arch faced in diaperwork of bright blue and green mosaics in a framework of brick, supported by elaborate limestone corbels. The pediment above all this is in blue and red brick and pierced by three tiny arches.

LEFT AND RIGHT
University Church,
St Stephen's Green, Dublin

variously described as Romanesque, Venetian, Renaissance and Lombardic, as well as noted as being 'one of the greatest masterpieces of the Gothic Revival . . . the finest secular building the movement ever produced'. The architects were principally influenced by the Venetian Byzantine revival of the late fifteenth and early sixteenth centuries, much loved by John Ruskin, who wrote to Deane expressing his 'high approval' of the plans when they were published. Dante Gabriel Rossetti, who had met Woodward in Oxford where the architect was supervising the erection of the Oxford Museum, called it '*the* building' to see in Dublin.

The importance of the entrance door is emphasized by the strong and richly decorated Venetian triple window above it, with its balustraded balcony acting as a canopy. The door and its sidelights are bordered by square pilasters, the capitals of which, like the other 102 capitals on the exterior of the building, are richly carved in different designs by the County Kilkenny stonemasons the O'Shea brothers. That on the left of the doorway depicts amid foliage two birds turned towards each other, and that on the right depicts a bird flapping its wings to steady itself as it feeds on berries in a composition of ivy, oak leaves and convolvulus flowers. The door is framed and panelled oak with copper fixings, and in the decorated stone tympanum above it the arms of Trinity College are displayed. The doorway pierces the richly decorated but very austere grey exterior to reveal a dramatic surprise: an entrance and stair hall ablaze with colour, an opulent space of marble columns and Byzantine arches topped by a double-domed tiled ceiling.

ABOVE, BELOW AND OPPOSITE
The Museum Building,
Trinity College, Dublin

Trinity College was founded in 1592 and modelled on the English universities of Oxford and Cambridge. The extant campus buildings, the oldest of which are eighteenth century, represent the best of the architecture of their periods, the Museum Building being no exception. Designed by the firm of Deane and Woodward, it is a pièce de résistance of Irish craftsmanship of the period, so rich in stylistic form that it has been

waterford city post office, 1879

During the Victorian period, Her Majesty's Post Office assumed a role as the most important agent of the British government, touching the lives of all classes and creeds through the services it offered, from mail to banking and from telegraphic communication to, eventually, a telephone service. A building that underlines this new importance of the post office, Waterford City Post Office, was built on the site of the old custom house, at the time the most imposing building on the mile-long Waterford Quay overlooking the River Suir. It was designed by James Ryan, and the treatment of the façades is inspired by images of the Venetian Renaissance popularized by John Ruskin, who at the time was Slade Professor of Art at Oxford. The austerity of the building's grey limestone is relieved by the avoidance of symmetry and the composition, proportions and variety of the window openings. The city of Waterford, besieged many times in its thousand-year history, was the last city in Britain or Ireland to come under siege, when the army of the Free State invested it during the Civil War in 1922. The post office, although damaged by shellfire, was saved from destruction when the Republican forces withdrew.

The customers' entrance, under a triple-bay Gothic portico, seems understated. The subject of this study, however, the carriage entrance, faces the main thoroughfare and the River Suir, and was given greater emphasis. Through its portals the mail vans, which had collected their important cargo at the railway station across the river, brought the local mail for distribution and the many postmen departed to make the final deliveries. This is a typical example of a doorway being used purposefully to make an announcement about a building. An uncomplicated Gothic arch in smooth limestone covers a tympanum-like stone panel bearing a richly carved royal coat of arms with two Latin inscriptions, translating as 'Evil to him who thinks evil', and 'Duty and my right'. The timber panel over the diagonal timber sheeted doors boldly bears the date of the commencement of building and the intertwined motif 'V.R.' for 'Victoria Regina', the whole underlining the importance of both the Royal Mail and the British Empire.

LEFT AND RIGHT
Waterford City Post Office

In some buildings of small scale, particularly shops, it is impossible to divorce the doorway from the display window, as in the case of the typical Irish Victorian small town or village shop. In former times there would have been little to distinguish a village shop from any other house in the village, as advertisement was not necessary in a small community. As places became more prosperous in mid- to late Victorian times, however, and there was more than one pub or shop in a village, display became important and a vernacular style developed, based on the large shops of the cities, using similar classical features, such as columns and pediments, but often stylizing them in an engaging, primitive way.

This shop has a panelled door, new, but probably to the pattern of the original, framed by stylized square pilasters topped with primitive Ionic capitals. The display window still retains its Victorian twin-paned glazing with elegant arched frames. A wrought-iron bar protects the glass from the herded horses or livestock of another time pressing up against it. It has long ceased to be a shop and is now a dwelling, but the decoration, complete with fascia advertising the name and trade, has been lovingly kept up.

LEFT AND RIGHT
Shop at New Ross,
Co. Wexford

the guildhall, derry, 1887

Derry's Guildhall is a magnificent Tudoresque Gothic concoction in rubble sandstone with old red sandstone dressings, built in 1887 to the designs of John Guy Ferguson. It was completed for £19,000 and paid for by the Honourable Irish Society of London. Formal City Council functions are held here, and visitors and dignitaries are entertained by the Lord Mayor in the Mayor's Parlour. The building was burned down in 1908; it was remodelled by M.A. Robinson and reopened in 1912. Bombed twice during the troubles, the building was refurbished yet again and reopened in 1977; somehow, the stained glass, amongst the finest in the British Isles, survived both bombings. The clock in the tower of the Guildhall, modelled on Big Ben in London, is the fourth largest clock in Ireland.

The entrance doorway and the tower above it is a survival of the original building by Ferguson. The doorway is deeply set back in a tall, slender and intricately decorated red sandstone Gothic arch: above it is a spandrel with three armorial plaques and three ogee-headed windows, all surmounted by an array of the arms of Londonderry. The arms depict a skeleton, signifying that the city was raised from the dead after it was sacked by Sir Cahir O'Doherty in 1608, and a castle, which indicates that the city is a walled city, indeed the last walled city to be built in Europe. The motto 'Vita Veritas Victoria' means 'Life, Truth and Victory'. Above the arch is a steep-sided pediment down which two lions crawl.

RIGHT AND OPPOSITE
The Guildhall, Derry

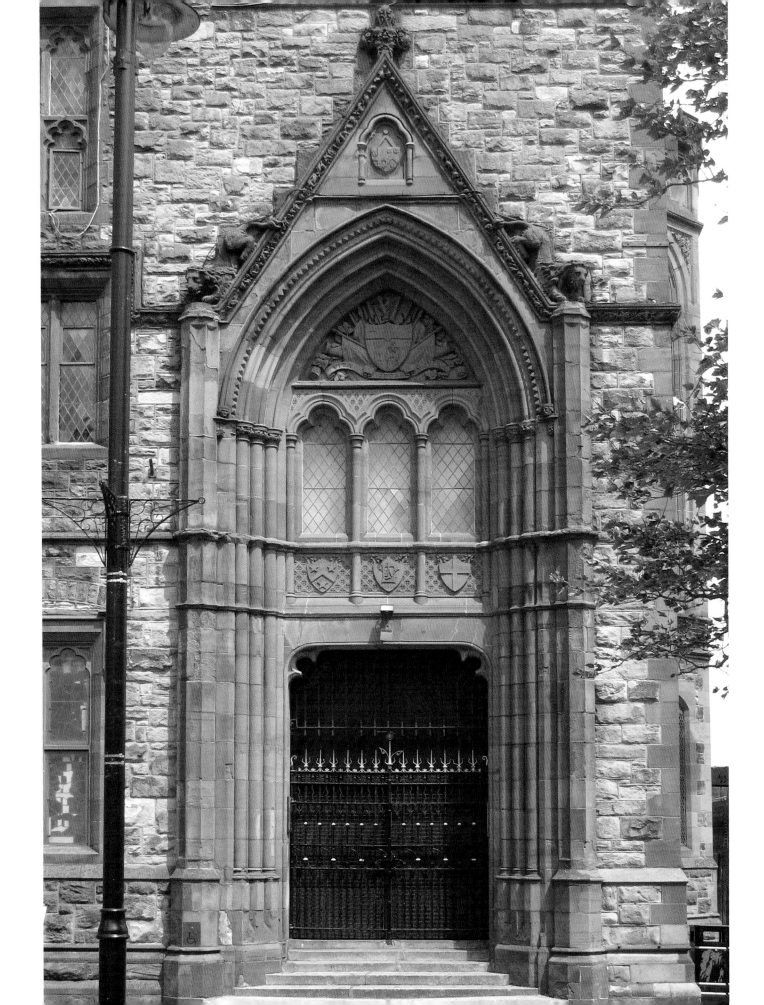

the honan chapel, cork, 1916

The Honan family were prominent merchants in Cork, and when the last member of the family died in 1913, a substantial amount of money was bequeathed for charitable and educational purposes. Some of that money was spent to provide a hostel for students, and the executor of the Honan will, Sir John O'Connell, also wanted a chapel to be built. He had strong ideas about the design of the chapel, believing it should be in the Hiberno-Romanesque style and built of local materials by local craftsmen. His wishes were carried out by the architect James McMullen of Cork, and the artwork and craftsmanship that set it apart were carried out by the leading artists, sculptors and craftsmen of the time, displaying the splendid state of survival of traditional crafts in Ireland in the early twentieth century. Internally, it is a feast of sculpture, mosaicwork and decorative glass, stone and timber.

The doorway, at the centre of an arcade of Romanesque arches, is a generous opening in pale grey carboniferous limestone, bordered by a deeply cut series of concentric arches decorated with traditional Romanesque motifs. There are strong similarities with the twelfth-century façades of St Cronan at Roscrea and Killeshin Church in County Laois (see page 28). On a corbel above the doorway is the sculpted figure of St Finn Barr, the patron saint of Cork. The oaken doors are hung on wrought-iron hinges of a design that is a fusion of Celtic and Art Nouveau. One enters the doorway past the heads of six Munster saints forming the capitals of the partly engaged layers or set-backs of columns flanking the doorway: these are exquisite works of the stonecarver's art, and indicate what the carvings on all Ireland's Romanesque churches must have looked like before they were blunted by atmospheric erosion. Strangely, the piers and gateway separating the chapel from the general university grounds, and the circular 'performance space' set in front of the recently completed adjacent Devere Hall, have no symmetric relationship to the chapel; and it is a pity that the architects of the later buildings that were built close by seem to have made little attempt to acknowledge this masterpiece.

LEFT AND RIGHT
The Honan Chapel, Cork

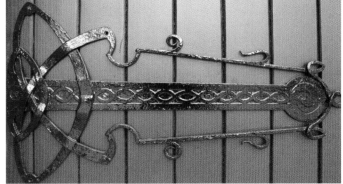

house at collon, co. louth. c.1920

Collon is a small but busy County Louth estate village on the old road north from Dublin. There are a number of fine traditional houses in the village, but in this fundamentally ordinary, plain early-twentieth-century terrace, one of the houses stands out and catches the eye.

The front door has been lifted far above its station with a frothy confection of wrought iron. It is not simply the ironwork that distinguishes this doorway: the delicately curved ogee arch form into which it has been crafted sets it truly apart. Iron is often thought of as weighty and crude, but these characteristics are more related to cast iron rather than this example, which is wrought iron in its lightest form. Cast iron, although more brittle, is made by pouring molten iron into a mould. Wrought iron, however, is pliable and forged hot by hand into a variety of shapes and designs. Painted white as this is, its very lightness is contrasted against even the window frames of the house. There is a considerable tradition of good-quality cast-iron and wrought-iron work in Ireland, mostly found in the cities and mostly related to distinguished buildings. In this case, a filigree-like screen of light flats has been made up using a simple but well-crafted spiral design: the transition between the stiles and the top has been particularly cleverly handled. The decorated doorway is approached along a short but formal path bordered by simple topiary, and statues of a pair of swans and a pair of maidens bearing baskets.

LEFT AND RIGHT
House at Collon, Co. Louth

the church of christ the king
turner's cross, cork, 1927

In a nondescript suburb of Cork city this remarkable example of 1920s Expressionism is quite a surprise when one comes upon it. It was designed by Barry Byrne, an American architect of Irish Catholic descent who had worked for Frank Lloyd Wright. This church is an important landmark not only in Irish architecture but also in the history of Expressionism in Europe. It is all the more remarkable in that the early-twentieth-century Irish Catholic Church was not known for its patronage of modern design ideas, but Byrne's initial plans were fully accepted without any alterations other than the suggestion that, for economy, the structure might be built in concrete, as it eventually was. On the completion of the church, however, Dr Coughlan, the Bishop of Cork and the client, seems to have been taken aback by its stark modernity and absence of traditional forms, and it was to be thirty years before another church in the contemporary style was built in Ireland.

In this angular, octagonal building, the western entrance façade is the most dramatic element. The elongated sculpted form of Christ the King by John Storrs seems to grow out of the façade and divides the entrance into two doorways. Forty-five-degree angles abound, with the surround of the entrance formed in serrated fairfaced concrete, set off by the contrasting ivory-tinted patent stipple that covers the rest of the structure. The angularity is carried through on to the ground plane, where a series of dark-toned concrete tiles, almost a shadow of the high façade overhead, lead to the entrance. The mahogany doors are tall and slender and repeat the diagonal motif. All this axial drama cries out to be properly viewed; probably because of a late change of site, however, this great façade does not face a long tree-lined boulevard but is shoehorned into a tight suburban location facing a small pub and a terrace of modest houses across an ugly ESB pole and wires.

ABOVE AND RIGHT
The Church of Christ the King,
Turner's Cross, Cork

106

LEFT AND RIGHT
The Church of Christ the King,
Turner's Cross, Cork

wendon, glasnevin, dublin, 1930

Relatively few good examples of work from the early International style of architecture survive in Ireland. Even before the development frenzy of the Celtic Tiger, many had already disappeared, including the Aspro Factory in Inchicore in Dublin and the Imco building in Merrion in Dublin, and few of those remaining have been appreciated and properly conserved. One of the first houses to form the vanguard of the International style in Ireland was Wendon in Glasnevin, Dublin, built for developer George Linzell, who was involved in the housing boom in Dublin in the late 1920s and early 1930s. While most of the houses Linzell built were of advanced design, they were not radically so, and he wanted to showcase in his own house the latest architectural ideas. It was designed by Harold Greenwood, a London architect, and completed in 1930. Wendon has a shallow V-shaped plan, and is considerably larger than later houses of this style in Ireland. Flat-roofed, it incorporated the latest European features, such as a ground-floor loggia at an obtuse angle, over which soared a substantial roofed balcony. In 1932 the *Irish Builder* magazine called Wendon 'Dublin's Wonder House'.

Wendon is no longer a private house, and is used today as a store by the Irish Fisheries Board. Although a little neglected, it has survived reasonably well. The entrance to the house is set in the acute angle of the V. The windows on the façades of the obtuse elevations, which face south and west, are large, while those on the façades of the acute angle, facing north and east, are considerably smaller. The entrance door, under a stylized canopy supporting three globe light fittings, is set deeply back into the façade with Art Deco receding side jambs in sand-

cement render. The door furniture is probably original, and the fretted glazing bars and stippled glass in the door itself, echoed on either side by those in the side windows, have survived. Greenwood paid tribute to classical architecture by including over the door a hint of a tripartite or Venetian window, the centre opening of which is topped by a blind, scalloped arch.

irishtown library, ringsend, dublin, 1932

Irishtown Library is one of the few Art Deco buildings to be built in Ireland, most of which were cinemas. Progressive Irish architects flirted with the style but did not entirely take to it, preferring to experiment with the more rigid disciplines of the International style. Dublin Corporation had the good fortune to employ a progressive coterie of architects through the mid-1920s into the 1930s, and their work, although not widely appreciated at the time, can be seen today to be of a very high quality. In the early 1930s, the Corporation Architect's Department was responsible for a series of small public libraries built in the new suburbs of Phibsboro, Drumcondra and Inchicore, and this example at Ringsend.

The designer would have been conscious of the high quality of the architecture employed during the previous period of library building earlier in the century for the Carnegie Foundation, and anxious that the building reflect the new thinking of the 1930s. The uncompromising modern character of the structure, two strong horizontal brick and concrete bands separated by a band of windows, is only slightly weakened by the steep pitched roof. The centrally placed and dominant doorway occupies a great block that slices through the horizontality of the rest of the structure: the scale of the block emphasizes the invitation to enter this public building, and the political and social importance placed at the time on literacy and the availability of books. This sense of importance is accentuated by the use of up-to-the-minute motifs of Art Deco expression in the decoration of the doorway, in the deeply faceted layer or set-back at the stiles and head, and in the chevrons framing the door opening.

LEFT AND RIGHT
Irishtown Library,
Ringsend, Dublin

Designed by London architect Harold Greenwood (see page 109), this one-off house at the entrance to the excellent Hampstead estate designed by the same architect stands out from all its neighbours. Unusually, it has survived unaltered, in its original form, for over seventy-five years, the only additions to its front façade being a burglar alarm box and some wiring. The design, which includes dramatic steeply stepped gable walls and a number of fine subtleties in the composition, displays a range of European influences. When asked to describe its style, architectural historian Brendan Grimes said that the strong green and white colours initially suggested to him a faintly Viennese Secessionist style, but he gave neo-Mannerist as a possible description.

The centre of the façade containing the doorway is subtly set back a few centimetres from the main façade, and extends up through the roof to form a gable in Tudor style. A window with a simple arched head and a flowing hood-moulding top the doorway, which is surrounded by a generous and elegantly moulded, shouldered and arched architrave in painted plaster. The door, a flush panel door with central lights, one of them decorated in bronze, takes up the form of the arched head over. The approach to the door is through a wrought-iron gateway on axis, and a path that bifurcates around a circular flowerbed to delay one's arrival at the door. The whole entrance is solidly grounded on a black bull-nosed brick stoup.

LEFT AND RIGHT
No. 1 Hampstead Avenue, Dublin

department of industry and commerce. kildare street. dublin. 1935

On the establishment of the Free State government in 1922 a new civil service was set up, employing many more people than had been previously involved in government work in Dublin. In the beginning, the new departments of state were scattered around Dublin in whatever accommodation could be obtained at short notice, until a new central office could be provided. The design for this building to house the Department of Industry and Commerce was the winning entry, by Cork architect J. Boyd Barrett, in an architectural competition held in 1935, but the building was not completed until 1942. It was the first and for many years the only Irish Free State government building designed and built specifically for its purpose. The result is a bold and accomplished design for a six-storey build-ing, the massing and proportions of which offer respect for the adjoining four-storey Georgian neighbours, as do the rusticated ground floor and slender windows, but it is emphatically a building of the 1930s, displaying Art Deco chevrons, zigzags and receding planes in a restrained but decisive way.

The entrance is a tour de force, emphasizing the impor-tance of the building and what it represents. The portal is surmounted by a carved limestone panel by the sculptor Gabriel Hayes, depicting the paraphernalia of modern industry, including aircraft, and the Celtic god Lugh overseeing the work of craftsmen. Above the panel, set back from the façade,

a limestone-framed glazed element soars five storeys to terminate in an arch, the keystone of which is a female head depicting Erin, recalling the heads representing the rivers of Ireland mounted on Dublin's Custom House. The wide double doors, set well back into the limestone portal, are robustly and regally decorated bronze.

LEFT AND RIGHT
Department of Industry and
Commerce, Kildare Street,
Dublin

st aengus's church, burt, co. donegal, 1967

Inspired by the great Grianan of Aileach crowning the hill above it (see page 14) St Aengus's Church at Burt is the work of the late Liam McCormick, whose churches, while finely and well thought out, are remarkably different from each other. His church at Burt echoes that at An Grianan with its solid circular battered walls of squared rubble masonry, but it transcends it in the roof, which hovers above a clerestory of stained glass atop the stone wall and then soars towards the sky to terminate in an off-centre but axially located, glazed lantern light over the altar. The interior is ablaze with the vibrant reds and blues of clerestory stained glass, but the eye is drawn to the light emanating from the free form of the lantern that floods the altar with light.

A shallow cobble-surfaced moat surrounds the building, and the doorway is reached across a slender slab bridge. The doorway is about strength and permanence: a deep fairfaced concrete canopy cantilevers out a metre beyond the wall to cover the wide opening. A pair of heavy bronze-sheeted doors with circular decorative handles give access to the interior. They are separated from the jambs of the opening by panels of frameless plate glass that reflect the landscape of Donegal and on which is inscribed in Gaelic text the names of those responsible for making the building.

LEFT AND RIGHT
St Aengus's Church, Burt, Co. Donegal

central bank, dame street, dublin, 1978

Dominating this street of mainly nineteenth-century buildings, the Central Bank was a controversial project from the beginning, its construction involving the creation of a wide gap in a central city street and the demolition of the Commercial Buildings, a fine granite-faced block that dated from 1799. Nearly thirty years on, during which many other dramatic contemporary buildings have followed it into the Dublin urban landscape, the Central Bank has become an accepted part of the city. It has an unusual structure, in that its seven office floors are suspended from the top of a central core rather than being supported in the conventional way on columns. This allows the considerable bulk of the building to seem to hover over a small public plaza which, except in bad weather, is thronged with passers-by and people seated on bulbous polished granite seats. A pastiche of the Commercial Buildings was built to the east of the bank, overlooking the plaza.

Entry to the building is by way of two smoked-glass rotating doors high above street level, which hang like two dark tubes from the coffered soffit of the projecting first floor. Duality in such elements always encourages a frisson of indecision in those approaching for the first time, and in this case the indecision will be accentuated by the pair of daunting splayed granite staircases of twenty-two steps to be negotiated before the entrance level is reached. In recent years railings and gates have been erected, which are effectively a further barrier to the entrance area. The dominance of the building and its disregard for the line of the street, combined with the sense of remoteness and inaccessibility suggested by its main entrance, could be seen as a subliminal comment on the hub of Ireland's banking industry.

LEFT AND RIGHT
Central Bank,
Dame Street, Dublin

the national gallery of ireland
millennium wing
clare street, dublin, 2001

This extension to the National Gallery was designed by the Scottish architects Benson and Forsyth, and completed in 2001. It takes the place of two fine Georgian houses that were allowed to fall into disrepair during the 1980s, and connects with the rear of the National Gallery, which fronts on to Merrion Square. As in many contemporary buildings, the main façade neither displays the structural form of the building nor gives clues as to what happens behind it. Instead, we have here a sculptural composition of elements, in panels of glass and Portland stone cladding, including a great vertical slab that hangs seemingly precariously in space for no reason that is easily apparent. A contemporary critic has described the style as 'a refined neo-Brutalist idiom informed by Scottish medieval architecture', which seems to sum it up quite well.

The entrance is little more than an insignificant slot, a dark, low rectilinear cave, at the ground level of one of the façade elements, consisting of an opening a mere 2.6 metres wide and a similar dimension high, with heavy doors set back 3 metres from the pavement. One would be excused for thinking that this is just another example of how entrances have been greatly reduced in significance in contemporary architecture, where often the entrance to the car park is treated with more importance than the main, pedestrian doorway. There is, however, a good reason for the scale of this doorway, a reason that harks back to those early Christian, narrow and low trabeate portals. It is all about drama: the visitor feels compressed entering the dark, low porch, only to heave back the heavy doors and be thrilled by the brightly lit space inside, a soaring cathedral-like entrance concourse that is a piece of sculpture in itself.

LEFT AND RIGHT
The National Gallery of Ireland Millennium Wing, Clare Street, Dublin

the glucksman gallery, cork, 2004

The Glucksman Gallery, designed by O'Donnell and Twomey, one of Ireland's foremost contemporary architectural firms, is sited in parkland beside the River Lee within the grounds of University College, Cork. It opened its doors to the public in October 2004. Housing exhibition spaces, lecture facilities, a riverside restaurant and a gallery shop, the gallery is named after American financier and philanthropist Lewis Glucksman, who began to take his vacations at Cobh, County Cork, in 1984, and subsequently lived there with his wife, Loretta Brennan Glucksman, from 1999 until his death in 2005.

Although of considerable bulk, the gallery rests lightly in its site, the upper section clad in American oak and supported on slender pilotis above a limestone base. It has been described as 'the best piece of public architecture in Ireland for decades'.

The entrance is in the undercroft of the upper section of the building, and an example of a doorway being reduced to the minimum necessary protection between the outside and the inside. The gallery is sited to the north of a wooded escarpment and the approach is across a generous limestone-paved causeway from the high ground to the first-floor level entrance. Entry to the building involves crossing the causeway and moving in under the curved form of the gallery floors to reach the interior. The importance of the doorway itself is reduced by its not being on axis with the bridge, and it consists of a pair of nondescript steel-framed glazed doors inserted into the glass box that is the entry level. It is as if the sense of entry, the portal aspect of entry, has been taken away from the actual doorway and invested in the bridge, which delivers you from the outside almost seamlessly into the interior.

LEFT AND RIGHT
The Glucksman Gallery, Cork

derry city council offices. 2005

Derry City's new council offices are a symbol of the Derry and Northern Ireland of the twenty-first century: forward-looking, optimistic and energetic. The offices are sited on the banks of the River Foyle, an icon in the history of the city. During the great siege of 1689 by the Jacobites under James II, the Protestant people of Derry were close to starvation when supply ships sent by William of Orange broke through a boom strung across the river, bringing food supplies and an end to the siege. A river landmark from a mile upstream and downstream, the new Derry City headquarters is the first in a series of modern commercial buildings currently under construction that reach north from the city towards the port as the concrete example of confidence in the city's future.

The main entrance to the building is on to a busy road, and it is signalled, but partly obscured, by a large canopy. The entrance that I have selected is on the river side of the building, overlooking a pleasant new linear waterside park. It is placed in a tall prismatic glazed breakfront that projects from the white limestone-clad main façade, and soars up to end in a louvred pediment above the building parapet. The glazed revolving door, housed in a brushed aluminium cylinder in brilliant metallic red, is reached by a wide flight of four stone steps. It is a welcoming entrance, an inclusive entrance, a declaration of a new future for the long-divided city. Beside the door an old anchor from a sailing ship is mounted, a symbol of those Williamite supply ships that ended the Jacobite siege and saved the city.

LEFT AND RIGHT
Derry City Council Offices

glossary

Acroterion: a decoration usually found at the foot or the apex of the pediment of a Greek temple.

Antae: side walls of a building, projecting, like pilasters, a short distance beyond the gable.

Anthemion: a decoration used in Greek and Roman architecture, based on the flowers or leaves of honeysuckle.

Architrave: a moulding surrounding or framing a doorway or window.

Arris: a sharp edge, a corner.

Batter: an inward inclination or tilt of a wall from its base upwards.

Breakfront: where the plane of part of the façade of a building is placed forward from the rest of the façade.

Bolection: a moulding used to cover a construction joint.

Bullaun: a rough boulder that has had a basin-like depression carved in it. Bullauns are most often found in ancient church sites but their origin and purpose is unclear.

Capital: the decorated or carved top of a column.

Clerestory: the upper level of the main walls of a church, pierced by windows.

Console: an ornamental projecting bracket or corbel.

Corbelled construction: a roof or vault formed by courses of projecting brackets of stone supporting further brackets above.

Crockets: in Gothic architecture, a carved ornament usually based on a curved leaf form.

Dentils: a decoration of small blocks, usually used in rows, resembling a row of teeth.

Diaperwork: a regular pattern carved on the surface of stone, derived from textile patterns.

Diocletian window: a window of semi-circular shape.

Egg and dart: a decoration in classical architecture consisting of alternate egg and arrowhead shapes.

Fairfaced concrete: a concrete surface that requires no additional treatment other than curing.

Fluting: a classical decoration of concave grooves in columns and pilasters.

Gibbsian: from a style employed by the eighteenth-century architect James Gibbs, using architraves interrupted by massive blocks.

Jamb: the vertical side of an opening in a wall.

Lintel: a structural member spanning over an opening in a wall.

Moulding: timber or stone that has been shaped into varied ornamental contours.

Ogee arch: an arch made up of concave and convex arcs.

Opes: openings in walls, usually for doors or windows.

Oriel window: a window projecting from the wall of the upper storey of a building.

Patera: a 'dish' or circular carved ornament.

Pediment: in classical architecture, the triangular end or gable of a building, but often referring to a triangular shape 'top' to other elements of a building.

Pilaster: a part square or circular column attached to a wall, usually 'engaged' – that is, built into the wall.

Pilotis: free-standing columns supporting a modern building.

Pinnacle: usually a decorative pointed feature terminating a vertical element.

Portal: a doorway or entrance, particularly one of an ornamental or imposing kind.

Pylon: a term from the Greek *pulon*, or gateway, often used in referring to the entrance to an ancient Egyptian temple.

Rusticated: masonry made up of massive blocks with deep joints between.

Sedelia: seating for the clergy in a church: in the medieval period usually built in masonry in the chancel wall.

Shouldered: an element such as an architrave which has been given additional emphasis at the corners.

Soffit: the underside of an element, usually a roof.

Spandrel: the space enclosed by an arch.

Swag: a carved ornamental festoon of flowers or foliage suspended at each end and hanging down in the middle.

Trabeate construction: from the Latin *trabs*, meaning a beam, an opening in a wall formed by using a flat lintel, rather than an arch form.

Tympanum: the vertical triangular space between the raking and horizontal edges of a pediment.

bibliography

The Buildings of Ireland series:

Casey, Christine, *Dublin*, Yale University Press, 2005

Casey, Christine, and Alistair Rowan, *North Leinster*, Penguin Books, 1993

Rowan, Alistair, *North West Ulster*, Penguin Books, 1979

Bence-Jones, Mark, *A Guide to Irish Country Houses*, Constable, 1988

Clarke, Mary, and Alastair Smeaton (eds), *Dublin's Georgian Squares,* Dublin City Council, 2007

Craig, Maurice, *Dublin 1660–1860*, Figgis, 1980

—, *The Architecture of Ireland from Earliest Times to 1880*, Batsford, 1982

De Breffney, B., and G. Mott, *The Churches and Abbeys of Ireland*, Thames and Hudson, 1976

Feehan, John, *Laois: An Environmental History*, Ballykilvan Press, 1983

FitzPatrick, E., and C. O'Brien, *The Medieval Churches of County Offaly*, Government Publications, 1998

Grimes, Brendan, *Irish Carnegie Libraries*, Irish Academic Press, 1998

Guinness, Desmond, and William Ryan, *Irish Houses and Castles*, Thames and Hudson, 1971

Gwynn, A., and R.N. Haddock, *Medieval Religious Houses of Ireland*, Irish Academic Press, 1988

Harbison, P., H. Potterton and J. Sheehy, *Irish Art and Architecture from Prehistory to the Present*, Thames and Hudson, 1978

Harbison, Peter, *A Thousand Years of Church Heritage in East Galway*, Ashfield Press, 2005

Killanin, Lord, and M. Guignan, revised and updated by Peter Harbison, *The Shell Guide to Ireland*, Gill and Macmillan, 1989

Lalor, Brian, *The Irish Round Tower*, Collins Press, 1999

Lanigan, K., and G. Tyler (eds), *Kilkenny: Its Architecture and History*, An Taisce, 1977

McManus, Ruth, *Dublin 1910–1940*, Four Courts Press, 2002

McParland, Edward, *Public Architecture in Ireland 1680–1760*, Yale University Press, 2001

Neeson, Eoin, *The Book of Irish Saints*, Mercier Press, 1967

O'Dwyer, Frederick, *The Architecture of Deane and Woodward*, Cork University Press, 1997

O'Keefe, Tadgh, *Romanesque Ireland*, Four Courts Press, 2003

Rothery, Sean, *A Field Guide to the Buildings of Ireland*, Lilliput Press, 1997

—, *Ireland and the New Architecture*, Lilliput Press, 1991

Royal Society of the Antiquaries of Ireland Journals, various

Stalley, Roger, *Architecture & Sculpture in Ireland 1150–1350*, Gill and Macmillan, 1971

Swinfen, Averil, *Forgotten Stones*, Lilliput Press, 1992

index